QUEEN
FOR UKULELE

ISBN 978-1-4950-8924-4

Another One Bites the Dust

Words and Music by John Deacon

First note

Intro
Steady Rock

3. There are

Verse

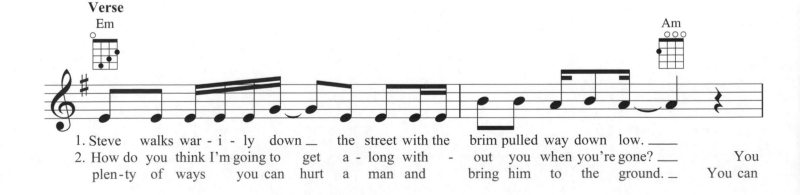

1. Steve walks war-i-ly down ___ the street with the brim pulled way down low. ___
2. How do you think I'm going to get a-long with-out you when you're gone? ___ You
   plen-ty of ways you can hurt a man and bring him to the ground. ___ You can

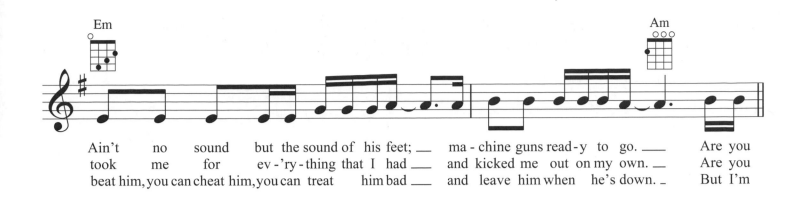

Ain't no sound but the sound of his feet; __ ma - chine guns read-y to go. __ Are you
took me for ev -'ry-thing that I had __ and kicked me out on my own. __ Are you
beat him, you can cheat him, you can treat him bad __ and leave him when he's down. __ But I'm

Pre-Chorus

read-y, hey! __ Are you read-y for this? __ Are you hang-ing on the edge of your seat? __)
hap-py? Are you sat - is - fied? __ How long can you stand the heat? __ }
read-y, yes, I'm read-y for you. I'm stand-ing on my own two feet. __)

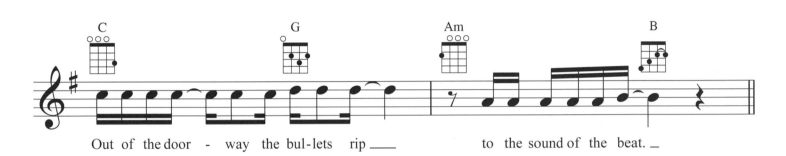

Out of the door - way the bul-lets rip ____ to the sound of the beat. __

Chorus

An - oth-er one bites the dust. __   An -

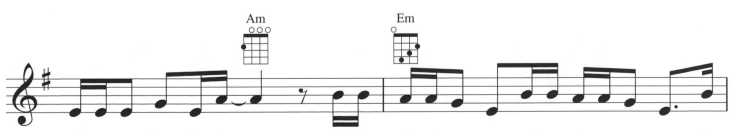

oth-er one bites the dust. __   And an - oth-er one gone, and an-oth-er one gone. An-

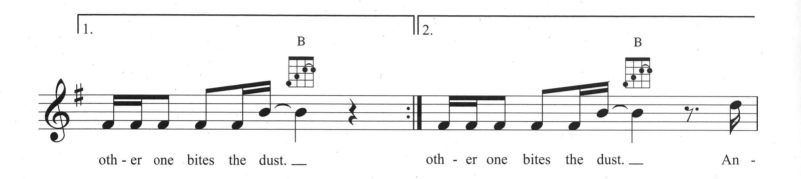

Bohemian Rhapsody

Words and Music by Freddie Mercury

mor - row,   car - ry   on,   car - ry   on   as   if   noth - ing   real - ly

mat - ters.

all.

Bridge
L'istesso tempo

I   see   a   lit - tle   sil - hou - et - to   of   a   man,   Scar - a -

mouche,   Scar - a - mouche,   will   you   do   the   Fan - dan - go?

Chorus:
Thun - der - bolt   and   light - ning,   ver - y,   ver - y   fright - 'ning

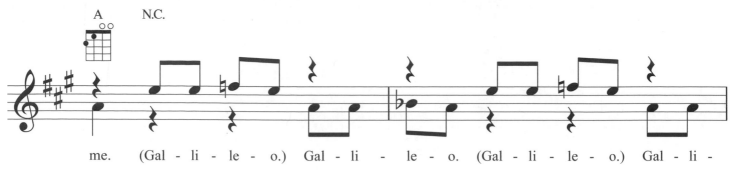

me. (Gal - li - le - o.) Gal - li - le - o. (Gal - li - le - o.) Gal - li -

le - o, Gal - li - le - o, Fig - a - ro, mag - ni - fi - co. _____

Solo: I'm just a poor boy and no - bod - y loves me.

Chorus: He's just a poor boy from a poor fam - i - ly.

Spare him his life from this mon - stros - i - ty.

Solo: Eas - y come, eas - y go, will you let me go? Bis -

Chorus:
mil - lah! No, we will not let you go. (Let him go!) ___ Bis - mil - lah! We

will not let you go. (Let him go!) ___ Bis - mil - lah! We

(Let me go!) ___ (Let me go!) ___
will not let you go. Will not let you go.

___ (Let me go!) ___
Will not let you go. Ah. ___

Solo: Chorus:
No, no, no, no, no, no, no. (Oh, ma - ma mi - a, ma - ma mi - a.) Ma - ma

here. —

Tempo I

Nothing really matters, anyone can see, nothing really matters,

nothing really matters to me. _____

Anyway the wind blows.

Crazy Little Thing Called Love

Words and Music by Freddie Mercury

Additional Lyrics

2. Well, this thing called love, it cries in a cradle all night.
   It swings, it jives, it shakes all over like a jellyfish. I kinda like it.
   Crazy little thing called love.

3. I gotta be cool, relax, get hip, get on my tracks.
   Take a back seat, hitchhike and take a long ride on a motorbike until I'm ready.
   Crazy little thing called love.

Don't Stop Me Now

Words and Music by Freddie Mercury

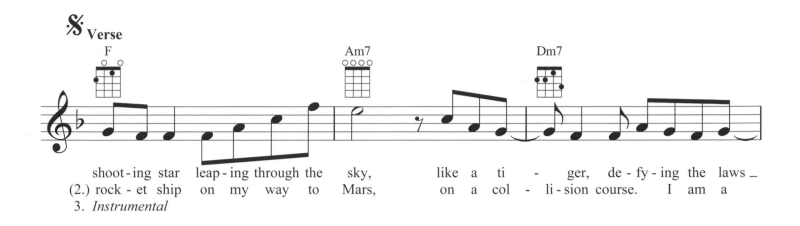

Verse

shoot-ing star leap-ing through the sky, like a ti - ger, de - fy-ing the laws _
(2.) rock - et ship on my way to Mars, on a col - li - sion course. I am a

3. *Instrumental*

___ of grav - i - ty. ___ I'm a rac - ing car, pass - ing
sat - el - lite; ___ I'm out of con-trol. I'm a sex ma - chine, read - y to re -

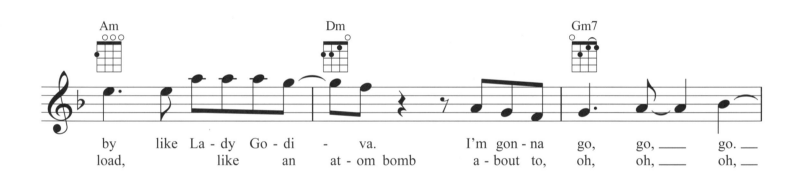

by like La - dy Go - di - va. I'm gon - na go, go, ___ go. _
load, like an at - om bomb a - bout to, oh, oh, ___ oh, _

Pre-Chorus

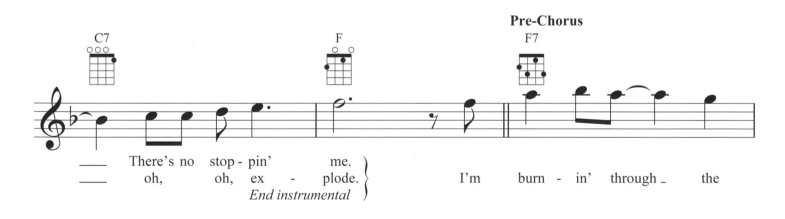

___ There's no stop - pin' me. I'm burn - in' through _ the
___ oh, oh, ex - plode. }
End instrumental }

sky, yeah. _ Two hun-dred de - grees, _ that's why they call me Mis-ter Fahr-en - heit. _

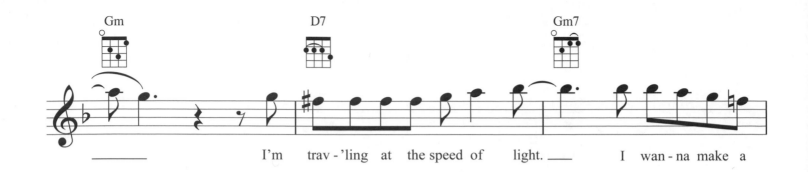

I'm trav-'ling at the speed of light. ___ I wan-na make a

To Coda 1 ⊕

Chorus

su-per-son-ic {man out / wom-an / man out} of you. ___

(Don't stop ___ me

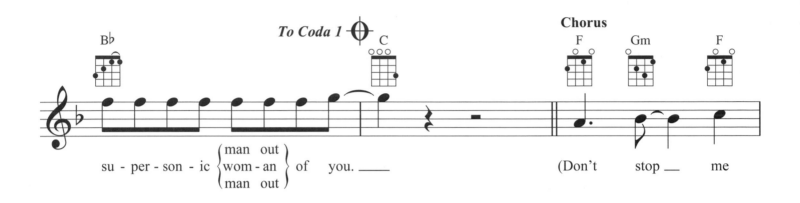

now.) I'm hav-in' such a good time, I'm hav-in' a ball. ___

(Don't stop ___ me now.) If you wan-na have a good time, just

give me a call. ___ 'Cause I'm hav-in' a good ___ time.
(Don't stop ___ me now.)

Yes, I'm hav-in' a good __ time. I don't wan-na stop at all. __

(Don't stop __ me now.)

_____

2. I'm a

Coda 1

__

Don't

stop me, don't stop me, don't stop me. Don't stop me, don't stop me, ooh, __

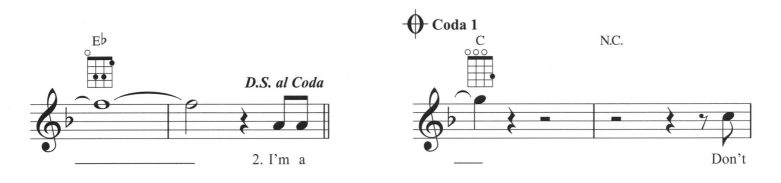

__ ooh, ooh. __ Don't stop me, don't stop me, have a good time, good time. Don't

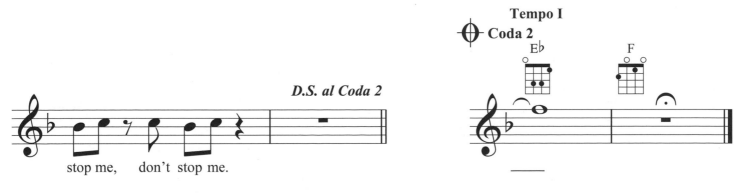

stop me, don't stop me.

__

I Want It All

Words and Music by Freddie Mercury, Brian May, Roger Taylor and John Deacon

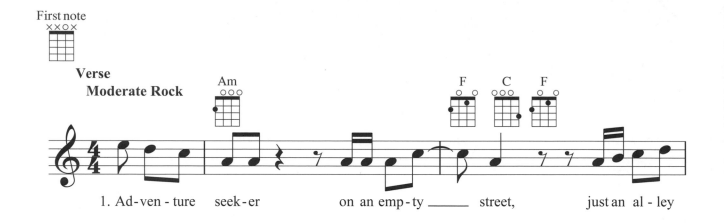

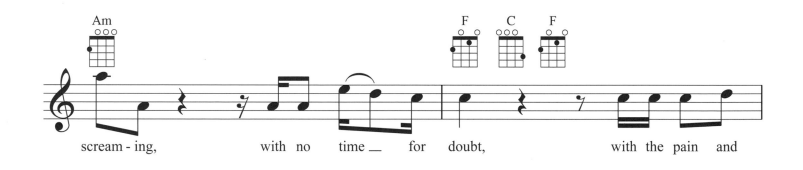

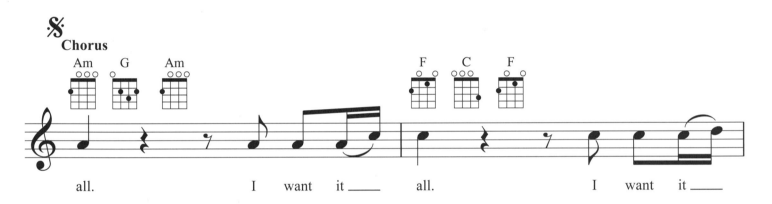

Coda

Bridge

I'm a man with a one-track mind, so much to do in one life-time.

Not a man for com-pro-mise and where and whys and liv-ing lies.

Yes, I'm liv-ing it all, and I'm giv-ing it all.

Coda 2

D.S.S. al Coda 2

It ain't much I'm

now.

I Want to Break Free

Words and Music by John Deacon

First note

I want to break free. _____ 1. I want to break

free.
(2.) love.
(3.) on.

I want to break free from your lies. You're so
I've fall-en in love for the first time; and
I can't get used to liv-ing with-out, liv-ing with-out,

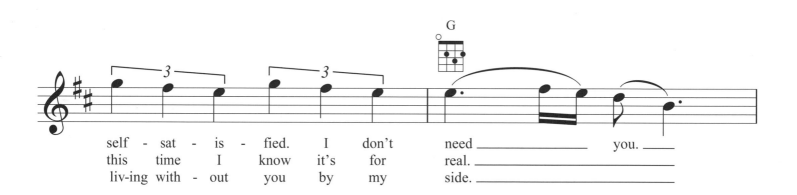

self-sat-is-fied. I don't need _____ you. ____
this time I know it's for real. ____
liv-ing with-out you by my side. ____

I've got to break free. __
I've fall-en in love, __ yeah. God
I don't want to live a-lone, __ hey. God
God

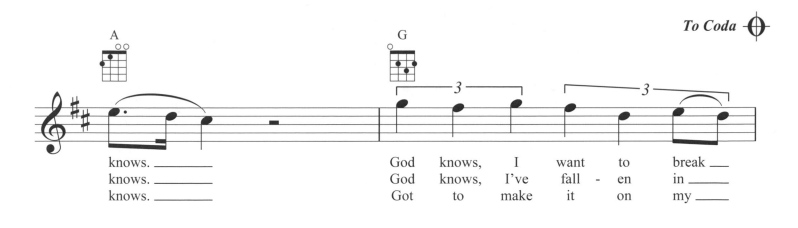

knows. _____ God knows, I want to break ___
knows. _____ God knows, I've fall - en in ___
knows. _____ Got to make it on my ___

free. 2. I've fall - en in It's
love.

Bridge

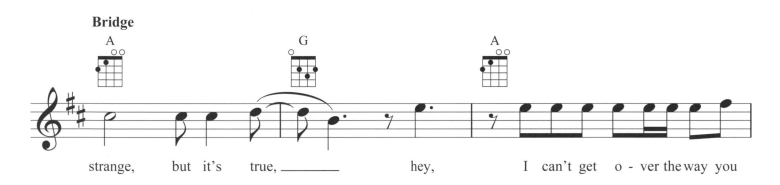

strange, but it's true, _____ hey, I can't get o - ver the way you

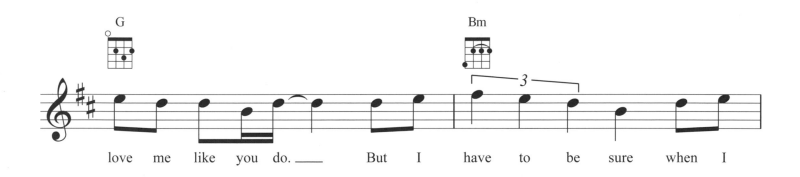

love me like you do. ____ But I have to be sure when I

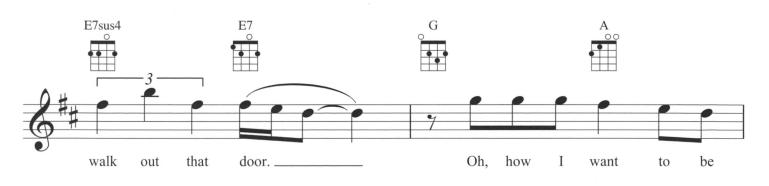

walk out that door. _____ Oh, how I want to be

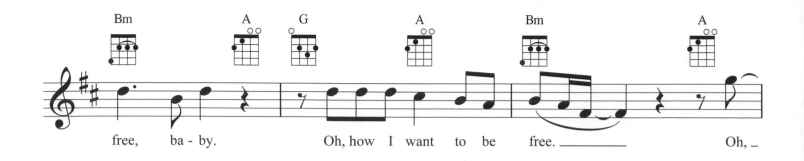

free, ba - by. Oh, how I want to be free. _____ Oh, _

_ how I want to break _____ free. _____ 3. But life still goes

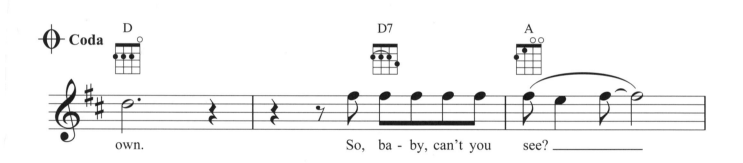

own. So, ba - by, can't you see? _____

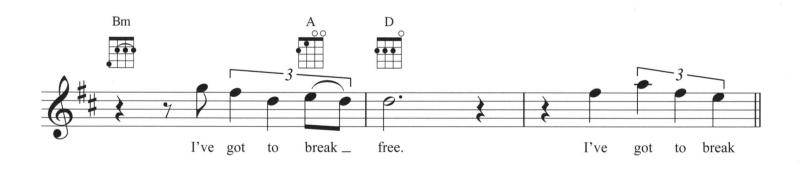

I've got to break _ free. I've got to break

free. I want to break _____ free. Yeah. _

Killer Queen

Words and Music by Freddie Mercury

well versed in et - i - quette, ex - tr'or - di - nar - i - ly nice.
cars she could - n't care ___ less, fas - tid - ious and pre - cise. } She's a

Chorus

kill - er queen, ___ gun - pow - der, gel - a - tine,

dy - na - mite ___ with a la - ser beam, guar - an - teed to blow your mind, ___

To Coda

an - y - time, ooh. Rec - om - mend - ed at the price, in -

sa - tia - ble an ap - pe - tite, wan - na try. ___

2. To a -

Radio Ga Ga

Words and Music by Roger Taylor

First note

%. Verse

Medium tempo

1. I'd sit a - lone ___ and watch your light, ___ my
(2.) gave them all ___ those old - time stars, ___ through
(3.) watch the shows, ___ we watch the stars ___ on

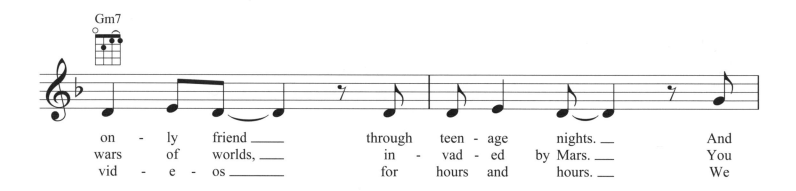

on - ly friend ___ through teen - age nights. ___ And
wars of worlds, ___ in - vad - ed by Mars. ___ You
vid - e - os ___ for hours and hours. ___ We

ev - 'ry - thing ___ I had to know, ___ I heard it on ___ my
made 'em laugh; ___ you made 'em cry. ___ You made us feel ___ like
hard - ly need ___ to use our ears. ___ How mu - sic chang - es

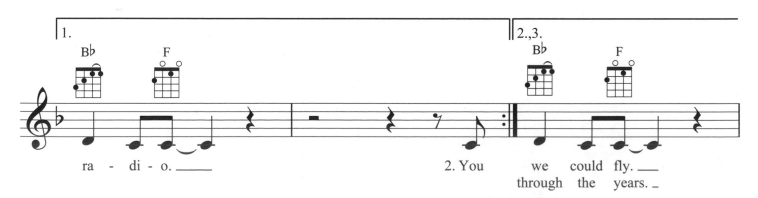

1.
ra - di - o. ___

2.,3.
2. You we could fly. ___
through the years. _

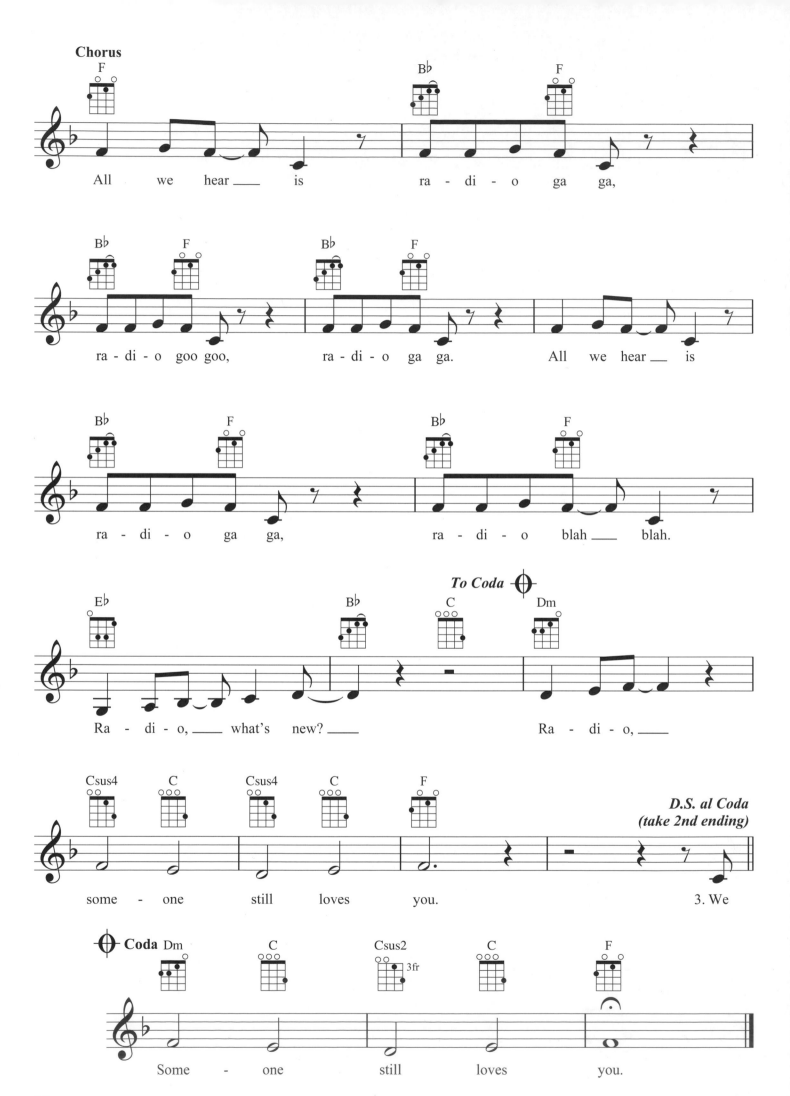

You're My Best Friend

Words and Music by John Deacon

Ooh, you make me live. _____ What - ev - er this world can
Ooh, you make me live. _____ When - ev - er this world is

give to me, _____ it's you, you're all I _____ see. _____
cruel to me, _____ I got you to help me for - give. _____

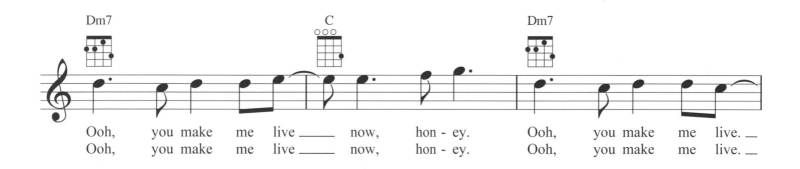

Ooh, you make me live _____ now, hon - ey. Ooh, you make me live. _
Ooh, you make me live _____ now, hon - ey. Ooh, you make me live. _

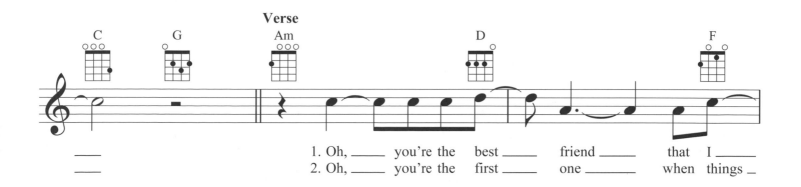

_____ 1. Oh, _____ you're the best _____ friend _____ that I _____
_____ 2. Oh, _____ you're the first _____ one _____ when things _____

___ ev - er had. __ I've been with you such a long time. __ You're my sun -_
___ turn out bad. __ You know I'll nev - er be lone - ly. ____ You're my on -_

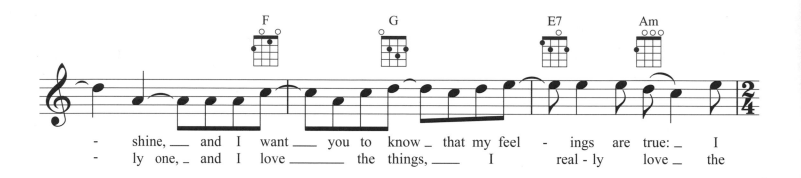

_\- shine, __ and I want __ you to know _ that my feel - ings are true: _ I_
_\- ly one, _ and I love _____ the things, __ I real - ly love _ the_

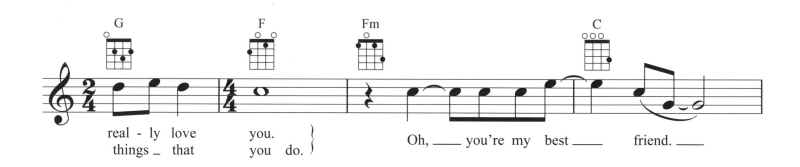

_real - ly love you. Oh, __ you're my best ____ friend. ___
_things _ that you do._

Bridge

_Ooh, you make me live. ____ Ooh, I've been_

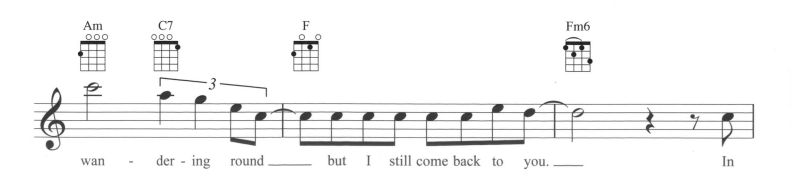

_wan - der - ing round _____ but I still come back to you. ___ In_

rain or shine, ___ you've stood by me, girl. __ I'm hap - py at home, __

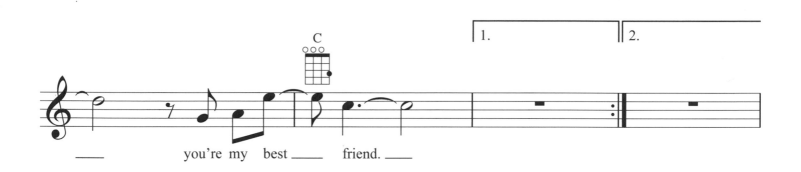

__ you're my best __ friend. __

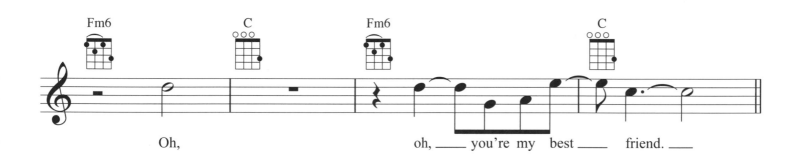

Oh, oh, __ you're my best __ friend. __

Outro

Ooh, you make me live. ___ Ooh, you're my best friend. __

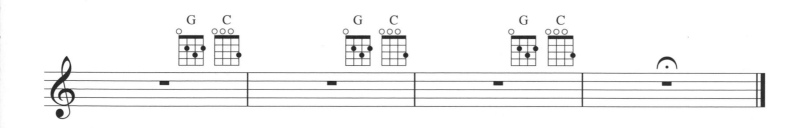

Save Me

Words and Music by Brian May

The Show Must Go On

Words and Music by Freddie Mercury, Brian May, Roger Taylor and John Deacon

Under Pressure

Words and Music by Freddie Mercury, John Deacon, Brian May, Roger Taylor and David Bowie

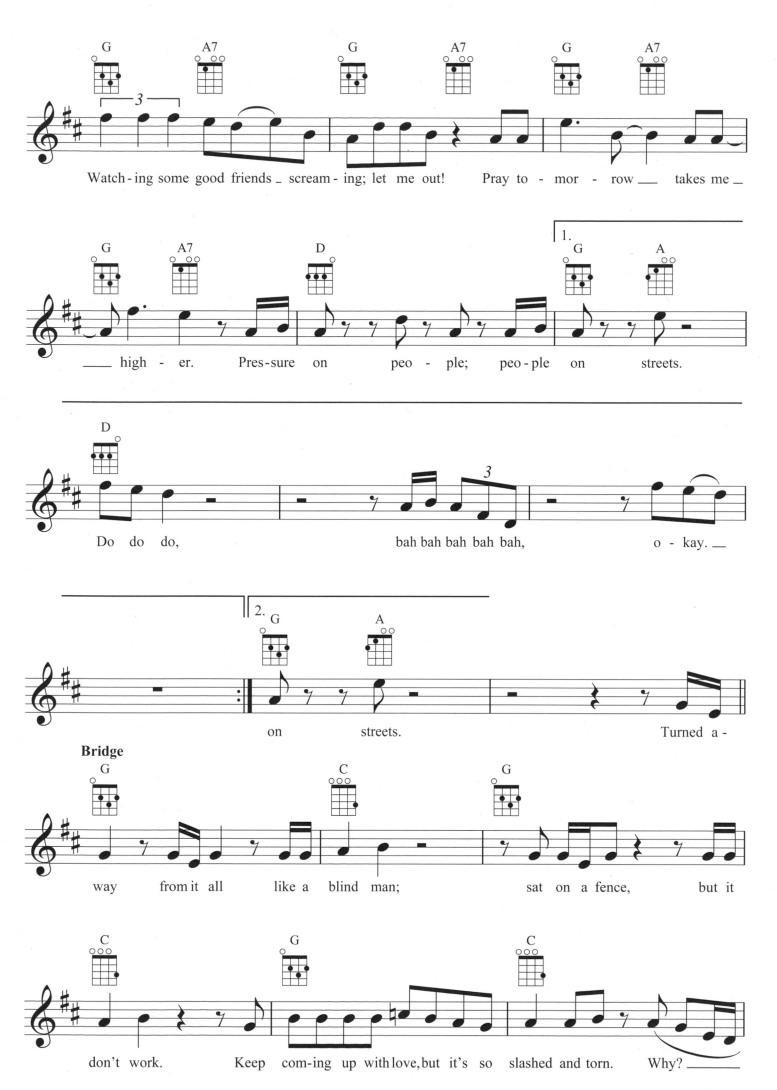

Watch-ing some good friends _ scream-ing; let me out! Pray to - mor - row __ takes me _

__ high - er. Pres-sure on peo - ple; peo-ple on streets.

Do do do, bah bah bah bah bah, o - kay. __

on streets. Turned a -

Bridge

way from it all like a blind man; sat on a fence, but it

don't work. Keep com-ing up with love, but it's so slashed and torn. Why? ____

43

word, and ____ love dares you ____ to care for ____ the peo - ple on the
edge of ____ the night, and ____ love dares you ____ to change our way of

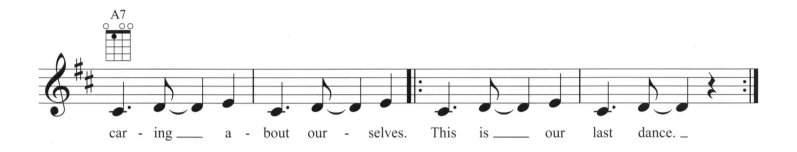

car - ing ____ a - bout our - selves. This is ____ our last dance. _

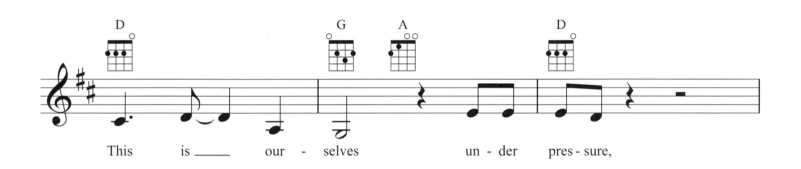

This is ____ our - selves un - der pres - sure,

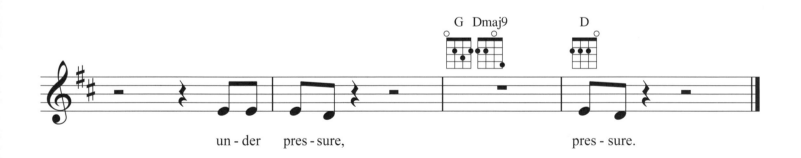

un - der pres - sure, pres - sure.

Additional Lyrics

2. Chippin' around,
   Kick my brains around the floor.
   These are the days it never rains but it pours.
   (Vocal ad lib.)
   People on streets.
   People on streets.

We Are the Champions

Words and Music by Freddie Mercury

We Will Rock You

Words and Music by Brian May

First note

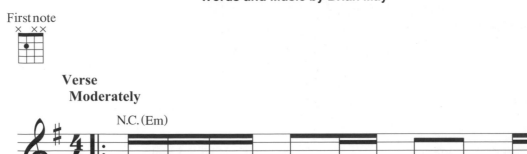

Verse
Moderately

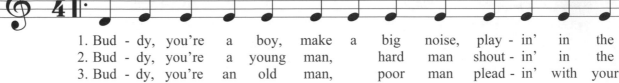

1. Bud - dy, you're a boy, make a big noise, play - in' in the
2. Bud - dy, you're a young man, hard man shout - in' in the
3. Bud - dy, you're an old man, poor man plead - in' with your

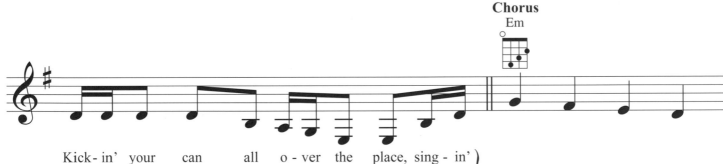

street. Gon - na be a big man some day. You got mud on yo' face, you big dis - grace.
street. Gon - na take on the world some day. You got mud on yo' face, you big dis - grace.
eyes. Gon - na make you some peace some day. You got mud on your face, you big dis - grace. Some -

Chorus
Em

Kick - in' your can all o - ver the place, sing - in' } we will, we will
Wav - in' your ban - ner all o - ver the place, sing - in' }
bod - y bet - ter put you back in - to your place, sing - in' }

1.,2.

rock you. ___ We will, we will rock you. ___ We will, we will

3.

We will, we will

C

rock you. We will, we will rock you. We will, we will rock you.